Silly Jokes & Giggles

By Philip Yates & Matt Rissinger

Illustrated by Ed Shems

STERLING

New York / London
www.sterlingpublishing.com/kids

To my darling daughters: Rebecca, Emily & Abby.

—Love, Dad

To my mom's cherished sisters and my precious aunts:
Annette, Dorothy, Maria, Marion, Mimi, Peggy Procko,
Peggy Yates, Rosemary, Vera, and of course, Aunt Marie
Gallen.

—Love, P.Y.

STERLING and the distinctive Sterling logo are registered trademarks of
Sterling Publishing Co., Inc.

Library of Congress Cataloging-in-Publication Data

Silly jokes & giggles / [compiled] by Philip Yates & Matt Rissinger ; illustrated by Ed
Shems.
    p. cm.
Includes index.
ISBN 1-4027-1075-5
I. Title: Silly jokes and giggles. II. Yates, Philip, 1956- III. Rissinger, Matt. IV.
Shems, Ed.

PN6166.S54 2005
818'.60208–dc22

                              2004028512

10 9 8 7 6 5 4 3 2 1

Published by Sterling Publishing Co., Inc.
387 Park Avenue South, New York, NY 10016
© 2005 by Matt Rissinger and Philip Yates
Distributed in Canada by Sterling Publishing
c/o Canadian Manda Group, 165 Dufferin Street
Toronto, Ontario, Canada M6K 3H6
Distributed in the United Kingdom by GMC Distribution Services
Castle Place, 166 High Street, Lewes, East Sussex, England BN7 1XU
Distributed in Australia by Capricorn Link (Australia) Pty. Ltd.
P.O. Box 704, Windsor, NSW 2756, Australia

Manufactured in the United States of America
All rights reserved

Sterling ISBN-13: 978-1-4027-1075-9 Hardcover
      ISBN-10: 1-4027-1075-5

Sterling ISBN-13: 978-1-4027-4071-8 Paperback
      ISBN-10: 1-4027-4071-9

For information about custom editions, special sales, premium and
corporate purchases, please contact Sterling Special Sales
Department at 800-805-5489 or specialsales@sterlingpub.com.

Contents

1 Let the Grins Begin!

FIRST MOTHER: How did you get your son to do sit-ups?
SECOND MOTHER: I just tied the remote control to his shoelaces.

JOE: I crossed a cell phone with a video game.
MOE: What did you get?
JOE: I don't know. Every time I try playing it, I get a busy signal.

From the Video Gamer's Bookshelf

Blurry Graphics, by Otto Focus

How to Pass the Time When Your Game Is Broken, by Rita Goode Booke

I Played Video Games Till Sunrise, by Emma Sue Tired

Video Card Games for One, by Sol A. Tare

Knock-knock!
Who's there?
Kenya.
Kenya who?
Kenya loan me some money to buy a video game?

HOLLIE: I crossed a video game with a microwave oven.
DOLLIE: What did you get?
HOLLIE: Really hot games that you can play in less than a minute.

Knock-knock!
Who's there?
Canoe.
Canoe who?
Canoe help me get to the next game level?

How can you tell if a video game is really old?
It has a sundial instead of a time display.

Knock-knock!
Who's there?
Manuel.
Manuel who?
Manuel be sorry if you don't read the instructions.

What do little fish do to pass the time?
Play eel-ectronic video games.

What do you get when you cross a video game with Dracula?
A program you can really sink your teeth into.

King Tut Video Game—Fun for the whole family
. . . even your mummy will love it.

What do you call a fruit that keeps bumping into trees?
A blind date.

You Know You've Been Playing Video Games Too Long When . . .

. . . instead of saying good-bye, you end your conversations with the words, "Game over."

. . . your parents take you to a restaurant, and you ask the waiter for a "pulldown menu."

. . . the microwave beeps and you yell, "Hey, best two out of three!"

Billy saw a flying saucer land in a nearby field. When the saucer door opened, a creature crept out. Billy could hardly believe what he saw. The alien had a big slimy mouth and twelve crooked yellow fangs. "I need to see your leader!" the creature demanded.

"Hmm," pondered Billy. "My dad is an orthodontist. Wouldn't you rather see him instead?"

Knock-knock!
Who's there?
Wooden.
Wooden who?
Wooden you like to come over and play video games?

Kooky Questions

How can you tell when you've run out of invisible ink?

If practice makes perfect, but nobody's perfect, why practice?

If swimming is good for your figure, how come whales are so fat?

What happens if you get scared half to death twice?

If you ate pasta and antipasto, would you still be hungry?

If a tree falls in the forest, do the other trees laugh at it?

When cheese gets its picture taken, what does it say?

BENNY: I don't understand. If an apple a day keeps the doctor away, what does garlic do?
LENNY: It keeps everyone away.

FIRST FRIEND: When I was just a little kid, I ran off with the circus.
SECOND FRIEND: Was it fun?
FIRST FRIEND: Before I could find out, the police made me bring it back.

Gags and Dolls

Did you hear about the baseball player doll? You wind it up at the store and it runs for home.

Did you hear about the Invisible Man doll? You wind it up and . . . "Hey, where did he go?"

Did you hear about the new shy-guy doll? You wind it up and it crawls back into the box.

Did you hear about the new workaholic doll? You can never unwind it.

What kind of doll swims really well and never needs winding?
A doll-phin.

Wife to absentminded professor: "Do you realize that fifty years ago today we were engaged?"

"Fifty years!" cried the professor. "You should have reminded me. We could have gotten married earlier."

DILL: What occurs once in a minute, twice in a moment, but never in an hour?
WILL: The letter *m*.

MINDY: What do you throw out when you want to use it, but take in when you don't want to use it?
CINDY: An anchor.

What goes up and never comes down?
Your age.

What question can you never answer "yes" to?
"Are you asleep?"

TEACHER: Can you spell your name backward, Simon?
SIMON: Nomis, I can't.

Why don't traffic lights ever go swimming?
Because they take too long changing!

DANA: Did you know that you can't take a picture of a
lady with a toaster?
LANA: Why not?
DANA: Because a toaster can't take pictures. You need
a camera.

What letter is never found in the alphabet?
The one you mail.

What do you get when you cross a lumberjack and Snow White?
Someone who is the forest of them all.

IGOR: Why was there thunder and lightning in the lab?
OGOR: The scientists were brainstorming!

The World's Top Ten Stupidest Inventions

10. Black highlighter.

9. Clear correction fluid.

8. Fake rhinestones.

7. Inflatable dartboard.

6. Glow-in-the-dark sunglasses.

5. Motorcycle air conditioner.

4. Sugarcoated toothpaste.

3. A system that allows you to report power failures via the Internet.

   And the Number One Stupid Invention?

1. A top ten list with just nine things!

What did the robot say when his battery went dead?
"AC come, AC go!"

Eduardo came in from playing in the mud and asked
his mother, "Who am I?"

Playing along with Eduardo, she replied, "I don't
know! Who are you?"

"Wow!" cried Eduardo. "Mrs. Herbert was right!
She said I was so dirty my own mother wouldn't
recognize me!"

What do you call a snowman in May?
A big drip.

Why did the old man run around his bed?
To catch up on his sleep.

What did the pine tree say to his girlfriend?
"I'm the one fir you."

What do you call a carousel with a watch?
A merry-go-wound.

2 Car-Har-Har!

What kind of car is good for people who can't remember the words?
A Hummer.

What do comics fill their cars with?
Laughing gas.

World's Worst Car Joke

A man went to his mechanic and complained that his car was always full of air bubbles and smelled like fish. The mechanic crawled in and pulled out a guy wearing a wet suit and scuba tanks.

"I think I found your problem," said the mechanic. "It's a backseat diver."

Benny was driving home one night when it suddenly started to hail. Soon there were tiny dents all over the car. When Benny stopped at an automotive garage to ask for help, the mechanic decided to play a practical joke on him. "Here's how you fix it," the mechanic said, trying to hold back his laughter. "When you get home, blow into the exhaust pipe as hard as you can and all the dents will pop out."

When Benny got home he did as the mechanic instructed. "What are you doing that for?" asked his friend Lenny. When Benny explained what the mechanic had told him, Lenny scratched his head and said, "You idiot! You have to roll the windows up first."

Bumper Sticker Funnies

GONE CRAZY; BE BACK SOON.

MONEY IS THE ROOT OF ALL EVIL—
SEND $9.95 FOR MORE INFORMATION.

GIVE BLOOD—PLAY HOCKEY.

I'M NOT DRIVING FAST, JUST FLYING LOW.

THERE'S NO FUTURE IN TIME TRAVEL.

AIR POLLUTION IS A MIST-DEMEANOR.

I HAVEN'T LOST MY MIND. IT'S BACKED UP ON A
DISK SOMEWHERE.

What did one tow truck say to the other?
"Are you pulling a fast one?"

CHICKIE: What's the difference between a book about
electricity and the rear light of a car?
DICKIE: One's a light tale, the other's a taillight.

What kind of performer can make vehicles talk?
A van-triloquist.

What's a mechanic's favorite part of the Sunday paper?
The car-tune section.

What do young truck drivers like most about school?
Study hauls.

What's the difference between a bat who gets around a lot and Bruce Wayne's car?
One's a mobile bat, the other's a Bat Mobile.

How do you get a frog off the back window of your car?
Use the rear defrogger.

SIGN AT A TOWING COMPANY
We don't charge an arm and a leg. We want tows.

SIGN OUTSIDE A TIRE REPAIR SHOP
Invite us to your next blowout.

SIGN AT A CAR DEALERSHIP
The best way to get back on your feet—
miss a car payment.

SIGN OUTSIDE A MUFFLER SHOP
No appointment necessary.
We hear you coming.

What extra do werewolves order for their cars?
A full-moon roof.

What does a frog do when her car breaks down?
Gets it toad and jump-started!

3 Pet's Entertainment!

Knock-knock!
  Who's there?
Venom.
  Venom who?
Venom we gonna get dinner?

Why aren't giraffes ever courageous?
They don't like to stick their necks out.

What did the mother worm say to the baby worm?
"Where in earth have you been?"

How do robins get in shape?
They do worm-ups!

DILL: I won ninety-three goldfish.
WILL: Where are you going to keep them?
DILL: In the bathtub.
WILL: But what will you do when you want to take a bath?
DILL: That's easy. I'll blindfold them.

My cat is so lazy, he pays the dog to chase mice for him.

What do dogs dislike about obedience school?
All the pup quizzes.

New Breeds of Dogs

A pit bull crossed with Lassie—she bites your leg off, then goes for help.

An Irish dog crossed with a telephone—golden receiver.

A K-9 dog crossed with the flu—germy shepherd.

How do rodents save each other from drowning?
With mouse-to-mouse resuscitation.

What grows up while growing down?
A goose.

Why did the horse cross the road?
To get to his own neigh-borhood!

What do you call a cow who works for a gardener?
A lawn moo-er.

MOTHER TEDDY BEAR: Would you like some dessert?
BABY TEDDY BEAR: No, thanks, I'm stuffed.

What kind of bee hangs out with witches?
A spell-ing bee.

MOE: What do you get when you cross a gambler and
an octopus?
JOE: I don't know, but it sure can play a lot of hands of
poker.

What do you call a bee in a rock band?
The lead stinger.

How do you keep a dog from barking in the backseat?
Put him up front and let him drive.

Who treats elephants with acne?
A pachydermatologist.

How does an elephant hide in the jungle?
She paints her trunk red and climbs a cherry tree.

What is gray and white on the inside and red and white on the outside?
An inside-out elephant.

JESS: What do you get if you cross a cat and a computer?
TESS: I'm not sure, but I bet it comes with a color purr-inter!

Where do mountain climbing pigs love to call home?
The Ham-alayas.

JEFF: I hear the three blind mice were lousy storytellers.
STEPH: That's because they had no tails to talk about.

Why did the dog go to the dry cleaner?
She had ring around the collie.

Where do they send stray dogs?
To an arf-anage.

Homer went to visit his friend Gomer and was surprised to find Gomer playing checkers with his dog. "That's amazing!" remarked Homer.
"Not really," replied Gomer. "He's lost every game but one."

FRANNY: What do you get when you cross a rubber band, a witch, and a dog?
DANNY: Snap, cackle, and pup.

ZED: What do you get when you cross a pit bull with an elephant?
NED: A very nervous postman.

IGGY: How can you tell when a snake is stupid?
ZIGGY: His head rattles more than his tail.

What's long, rattles, and eats pickled peppers?
Peter Viper.

KYLE: How do you train an electric fish?
LYLE: You put him on a leash and shout, "Eel!"

What stone-carved national mountain monument
honors presidential pooches?
Mutt Rushmore.

4 Punnies from Heaven

NED: I crossed an oven with an ATM machine.
TED: What did you get?
NED: Very crisp bills.

How do mermaids decorate their tails?
With sea-quins.

Who steals from the rich by day but skips off to visit his sick granny at night?
Little Red Robin Hood.

What sticky villain in Sherwood Forest keeps all the pancakes for himself?
The Syrup of Nottingham.

What Robin Hood sidekick loved fast food?
French Friar Tuck.

What do you get when you cross Robin Hood with a ghost?
Somebody very good with a boo and arrow.

Two cement mixers got married and now they have a little sidewalk running around the house.

Knock-knock!
Who's there?
Harley.
Harley who?
Harley any time left to go for a ride.

What famous pirate had to brush his teeth and be in bed by eight o'clock?
Captain Kidd.

What condition do you get when you cross an angel and a fiery devil?
Harp-burn.

What do you call a two-thousand-year-old flower wrapped in cloth strips?
A chrysanthe-mummy.

A Hairy Riddle

What's the difference between an orphan, a man with no hair, a baby gorilla's mother, and a king's son?

An orphan has nary a parent, a bald head has no hair apparent, a mother ape is a hairy parent, and a prince is an heir apparent.

What's the difference between a knight and Rudolph the Red-Nosed Reindeer?

One's a dragon slayer, the other's a sleigh dragger.

What do you get when you cross a silly bear with a springy toy?

A Pooh-go stick.

At the amusement park, Henry stepped forward and plopped his money at the ticket booth. "I want to go on the Mission to the Moon ride."

"Sorry," said the attendant. "The moon is full right now."

At the amusement park, Henry stepped forward and plopped his money at the ticket booth. "I want to go on the Skunk Hollow Hoe-Down Ride."

"Sorry," said the attendant. "That ride is out of odor."

ABSENTMINDED PROFESSOR: Honey, where are my shoes?

WIFE: They're on your feet.

ABSENTMINDED PROFESSOR: You're right. It's a good thing you saw them, or I would have left home without them.

DAFFY: My family is like a box of chocolates.

LAFFY: How's that?

DAFFY: They're pretty sweet, except for a few nuts.

What do you get when you cross James Bond with a bagpipe?

A spy with a license to kilt.

Little Jimmy was walking to breakfast wearing one sneaker.

"Have you lost a shoe?" asked his dad.

"Gosh, no," replied Jimmy. "I just found one."

Quickie Questions

If you crossed an elephant with a goldfish, would you get swimming trunks?

When Volkswagens retire, do they go to the old Volks' home?

If superheroes are so clever, why do they wear their underpants outside their trousers?

What U.S. president was trampled by an elephant?
George Squashington.

FIRST MATCHBOOK: What's new?
SECOND MATCHBOOK: Flame old thing.

What do you get when you cross three tenors and April 1st?
Opera Fool's Day.

What cereal is a favorite with young magicians?
Trix.

How did the paleontologist feel at the end of a long day?
Bone tired.

What do you get when you cross Robin Hood with a snake charmer?
Someone who is good with a boa and arrow.

MOM: How can you practice your trumpet and listen to the radio at the same time?

SON: Easy. I have two ears!

MOE: You ought to go to Hollywood!

JOE: Why?

MOE: The walk would do you good.

What ancient dinosaur used to terrorize everyone at breakfast?

Tri-cereal-tops.

Say These Three Times Quickly

The wild wind whipped Walt from the wharf.

If Roland Reynolds rolled a round roll 'round a round room, where's the round roll that Roland Reynolds rolled 'round the room?

WIFE: Honey, there's a bill collector on the phone. I told him you were out, but he wouldn't believe me.

ABSENTMINDED PROFESSOR: Oh, all right, give me the phone. I'll tell him myself.

Knock-knock!

Who's there?

Musket.

Musket who?

Musket my jacket—it's freezing outside.

Diaper Dillies

A baby snake's underwear—viper diaper.

Overactive underwear—hyper diaper.

Computer keyboard underwear—typer diaper.

Well-dressed baby underwear—dapper diaper.

Underwear that complains a lot—griper diaper.

A diaper made out of paper plates—dish-posable diaper.

MOM: What do you charge for children's photographs?
PHOTOGRAPHER: Twenty dollars a dozen.
MOM: I'll have to come back. Counting the twins I only have ten.

Knock-knock!
Who's there?
Wilda.
Wilda who?
Wilda movie be on TV tonight?

Knock-knock!
Who's there?
Ireland.
Ireland who?
Ireland you a dollar if you promise to pay me back.

Wickedly Wacky

How do poor candles survive?
On a wick-to-wick basis.

Where do candles go on vacation?
To the wax museum.

How did the candle know he was in love?
He met his perfect match.

What do you get when you cross a candle with a beach bum?
A self-waxing surfboard.

HOMER: Did you notice that candles cough a lot?
GOMER: That's because they start smoking at an early age.

What kind of candle can't lift a dumbbell?
A ten-pound wick-ling.

What did one candle say to the other candle?
Let's go out tonight!

Why did the cook add candles to the recipe?
He was trying to make a light snack.

Why do candle trimmers work so few days a week?
They only work on wick-ends!

TED: Every five minutes I break into song.
ZED: You wouldn't have to break in if you found the right key.

CASTLE PAGE #1: Is Sir Lancelot going on a long journey?
CASTLE PAGE #2: Why do you ask?
CASTLE PAGE #1: I just saw him packing his over-knight bag.

What do you call a giant caught in a rainstorm?
The Big Dripper.

MO: How did Aquaman become famous?
JO: He went to Hollywood and made a big splash.

What did the bee say after a long trip away from his house?
"Honey, I'm home."

What cartoon character loves to stretch and meditate?
Yoga Bear.

Why do nine out of ten roosters have little duck decals on their alarm clocks?
So they can get up for work at the quack of dawn.

Knock-knock!
Who's there?
He-Man.
He-Man who?
He-Man, isn't it time for school?

Mother Goose Graffiti

HUMPTY DUMPTY WAS CRACKED EVEN BEFORE HE FELL!

JACK AND JILL WERE PUSHED!

LITTLE MISS MUFFET ALWAYS CRIES WHEN SHE DOESN'T GET HER OWN WHEY.

MARY HAD A LITTLE LAMB, BUT SHE OVERCOOKED IT.

What kind of rhymes and poems are read at tree nurseries?
Mother Spruce.

What frontiersman loved to slow-simmer possum stew?
Davey Crock-Pot.

What caped crusader was known to disguise himself as a tree?
Spruce Wayne.

More Kooky Questions

Why do fat chance and slim chance mean the same thing?

Are hungry crows ravenous?

If a rabbit's foot is so lucky, what happened to the rest of the rabbit?

If a book called *How to Be a Failure* doesn't sell, does that mean it's a success?

We know the speed of light—so what's the speed of dark?

How does the guy who drives the snowplow get to work?

How do sheep know if you're pulling the wool over their eyes?

How do "DON'T WALK ON THE GRASS" signs get there in the first place?

What was the best thing *before* sliced bread?

Do hotcakes really sell like hotcakes?

Cinderella Sillies!

What do you call a beach blanket beauty wearing glass slippers?
Sand-erella.

What do you get when you cross a jolly man in a red suit with glass slippers?
Santa-rella.

What do you call a baseball official wearing a striped shirt and glass slippers?
Ump-erella.

What do you call a shark with glass slippers?
Fin-derella.

What's the difference between Cinderella and a gardener?
One has glass slippers, the other has grass snippers.

What do you call a spider wearing glass slippers?
Spin-derella.

What do you call a very, very skinny girl wearing glass slippers?
Thin-derella.

Who does an oyster call to get around town?
A taxi crab.

What great cartoonist loved to dance?
Waltz Disney.

What do you call a clock that can add, subtract, multiply, and divide?
A cookoo-lator.

What fur-loving lady villain works in a drugstore?
Cruella De Pill.

Letter from young Maid Marian at summer camp:
"Dear Mom and Dad, the days are okay, but I'm having trouble with the Knights."

Wedding Wackies

What do they toss at cats' weddings?
White mice.

What do bakers toss at an upsetting wedding?
Their cookies.

What do they toss at a bungee jumper's wedding?
The bride and groom.

What song does the organist play at mosquitoes' weddings?
"Here Comes the Bite."

What's the difference between someone who holds the wedding bands and a waitress at a fried chicken shop?
One's a ring bearer, the other's a wing bearer.

What's a ghost's favorite part of the wedding?
Trying to catch the bridal boo-quet.

What are two things a giant can't eat for breakfast?
Lunch and dinner.

What's a squirrel's favorite TV station?
The Cartoon Nut-work.

What would you get if you crossed a stuttering pig with a mummy?
Looney Toombs.

DANA: Did you enjoy the cartoon about the gummy monster?
LANA: It stuck with me long after it was over.

How do prisoners make calls?
On their cell phones.

What superhero loves dressing up in department store windows?
Spider-Mannequin.

Where does a guy who is able to leap tall buildings and is faster than a locomotive shop for groceries?
A super-market.

Why was the absentminded cartoonist fired from his job?
He drew a blank.

What buggy cartoon superhero keeps getting washed off buildings?
The Inky-Dinky Spider-Man.

5 Works 4 Me!

Who can shave twenty-five times a day and still have a beard?
A barber.

What do hockey players listen to?
Anything on a com-puck disc player.

A sailor was ordered to clean the chains on the ship's anchor. As she pushed the broom across the anchor, a tern appeared and landed on her head. "Shoo!" shouted the sailor to the tern, and finally, in anger, she grabbed the bird and tossed it overboard. A few minutes later, the tern reappeared, and the sailor again threw the annoying bird overboard.

The next morning, the chief petty officer checked out the sailor's work. "What's the big idea?" said the officer. "I told you I wanted those anchor chains spotless!"

"I couldn't help it," said the sailor. "I tossed a tern all night, but I couldn't sweep a link."

What's the difference between someone who keeps ships safe and someone who cleans up after the president?
One's a lighthouse keeper, the other's a White House sweeper.

MACK: I hear your father's chair factory went out of business.
JACK: Yes, they folded yesterday.

MOE: Do you think I'll reach my dream of becoming a trapeze artist?
JOE: Depends on whether or not you get the hang of things.

What kind of cameras are a favorite with sewer workers?
Ditch-ital cameras.

What do Alaskan explorers hate the most about going to work?
Getting caught in mush-hour traffic.

JOB INTERVIEWER: This job pays fifty bucks a week.

JOB APPLICANT: Why, that's a weekly insult!

JOB INTERVIEWER: Yes, but we only pay every two weeks.

JOB APPLICANT: All right, I'll take it, if it means I'll only be insulted twice a month.

SNIP: I broke all my teeth in carpentry school.

SNAP: How did you manage that?

SNIP: Chewing my nails.

What did the karate expert say to her boyfriend?
"Only thirty chopping days 'til Christmas!"

GROCERY CLERK: Does the manager know you knocked over all these cans of tomatoes?

STOCK BOY: I'm not sure if he does now, but the guys from the ambulance squad said he should start remembering things in about twenty-four hours.

FUZZY: Why can't you keep a secret in a bank?
WUZZY: Because of all the tellers.

Why did the fire-breathing woman quit the circus?
She was burned out.

What would you get if you crossed a lumberjack and a librarian?
Someone who spends all day leafing through books.

How do plumbers stay in touch over the Internet?
In-sink messaging.

Hardworking Farmer's Motto

No Pain, No Grain.

WINNY: Why were you kicked out of ballet school?
VINNY: I stepped on too many toes.

TIP: Why did the monkey run away from the man with the organ?
TOP: Every day it was the same old grind.

FLOYD: What would you get if you crossed a chili pepper with a washed-up comic?
LLOYD: A hot time in the old clown tonight.

DUMB COWBOY #1: What's that rope for?
DUMB COWBOY #2: Catching cattle.
DUMB COWBOY #1: What do you use for bait?

Light Laughs

How many car wreckers does it take to change a lightbulb?

Eight—one to change the bulb and seven to smash the old one to pieces.

How many mystery writers does it take to change a lightbulb?

Two—one to screw it almost all the way in and one to give it a surprising twist at the end.

How many movie directors does it take to change a lightbulb?

One, but he wants to do it fifty times.

How many spies does it take to change a lightbulb?

Sorry, I can't tell you. It's top secret.

The dumbest cowboy in the world went to an insurance office to get a policy.

"Did you ever have any accidents?" asked the insurance agent.

"No, siree!" replied the cowboy. "But one time a horse kicked me in the head and a rattlesnake bit me on the toe."

"Don't you call those accidents?"

"Why, heck no, mister! They did it on purpose."

SLIM: The first cattle ranch I ever worked at made a real impression on me.

JIM: So you learned a lot there?

SLIM: No, I backed into a branding iron.

Bumbling Business

"How's business at the candle factory?"
"It's starting to taper off."

"How's business at the coffin factory?"
"We're dead broke."

"How's business at the perfume factory?"
"We lost every scent."

"How's business at the rocket factory?"
"Everyone got fired."

"How's business at the duck factory?"
"It's got so bad we had to mark everything 'Down.'"

"How's business at the lemon-drop factory?"
"Things couldn't be bitter."

How does a fortune teller know if your job is setting up pins?
She gazes into her crystal bowling ball.

Did you hear about the two satellite repair technicians who got married?
The ceremony was awful, but the reception was excellent.

Vinny walked into the grocery store and said to the produce clerk, "I want all the rotten tomatoes you have."

"What do you want with rotten tomatoes?" said the grocery clerk. "Unless you're going to see that new comic who's appearing in town this week."

"I am the new comic," replied Vinny.

JOB INTERVIEWER: We're looking for someone who is responsible.

JOB APPLICANT: That's me. In my last job, whenever something went wrong, the boss said I was responsible.

COWBOY TO DWEEB: Why are you putting that saddle on the reverse way?

DWEEB: I want to ride back to the time of the Old West.

What do you get when you cross a barbershop with an ocean liner?
A clipper ship.

What do photographers and bats have in common?
They both hang out in dark rooms.

How do you know an undertaker is married?
In the bathroom you see His and Hearse towels.

From Gags to Stitches!

PATIENT: Doctor, Doctor, I think I'm a battery.
DOCTOR: How do you feel about that?
PATIENT: Well, it has its pluses and minuses.

What do you get when you cross a psychiatrist and a plumber?

I don't know, but it sounds like emotionally draining work.

Did you hear about the marathon runner who worked as a chimney sweep? She was a great runner, but she suffered from athlete's soot!

PATIENT: Doctor, Doctor, I feel like a pack of cards!
DOCTOR: I'll deal with you later!

PATIENT: Doctor, Doctor, I feel like a pair of curtains!
DOCTOR: Well, pull yourself together then!

What did the elevator operator say to his doctor?
"I think I'm coming down with something!"

What did the doctor say to the chimney?
"You'd be better off if you quit smoking!"

Take as Directed

Rude people with headaches take—crass-pirin.

Fishermen with headaches take—bass-pirin.

Colorful snakes with headaches take—asp-irin.

Heavy smokers with headaches take—gasp-irin.

Ghosts with headaches take—Casper-in.

Cats with headaches take—as-purr-in.

How come frogs don't need psychiatrists?
Because they eat what bugs them.

The absentminded professor had to be rushed to the hospital for chest pains.

"Professor," said the nurse, "the doctor is here to see you."

"Tell him to come back tomorrow," said the professor. "I'm too sick to see anybody right now."

PATIENT: Doctor, Doctor, you must help me. Every night I dream there are horrible slimy monsters under my bed. What should I do?

DOCTOR: Why don't you try sawing the legs off your bed?

PATIENT: Doctor, Doctor, I think I'm a cartoon character.

DOCTOR: Now that you mention it, you do look a little drawn.

Why did the leopard go to the doctor?
For a spot check.

The maternity nurse told the absentminded professor, "It's a boy, sir."

The professor said, "A boy? Well, what does he want? Tell him I'm busy right now."

The maternity nurse told the absentminded professor, "Congratulations! You've just become the father of a baby girl."

The professor replied, "Please don't tell my wife. I want it to be a surprise."

The absentminded professor's best friend congratulated him. "I hear your wife had twins. Boys or girls?"

"One is a boy and one is a girl," said the professor proudly. "Or is it the other way around . . . ?"

PATIENT: Hey, Doc, how long will I live?
DOCTOR: Don't worry, you'll live to be ninety.
PATIENT: But I just turned ninety today.
DOCTOR: See, what did I tell you?

When Chuckie thought he had swallowed a coin, his parents took him to the doctor. The doctor gave Chuckie an anesthetic, and when Chuckie woke up, the doctor was standing beside his bed, holding the coin.

"There's nothing more to worry about," said the doctor. "We operated on you and took out the silvery coin with George Washington's face on it."

"This is no time for coin tricks," said Chuckie. "The one I swallowed was brown and had Abraham Lincoln on it."

What does the doc prescribe for snakebite?
Anti-hiss-tamines.

PATIENT: Doctor, Doctor, I think I'm a coin-minting factory!
DOCTOR: Please, please, stop making cents.

Why did the wacky doctor send the stressed-out teapot to anger management classes?
To blow off a little steam.

Sign in a Dentist's Office

BE TRUE TO YOUR TEETH, OR THEY WILL BE FALSE TO YOU.

MOE: Did you hear about the giant monster who swallowed William Shakespeare and Stephen King and wound up in the hospital?
JOE: What happened?
MOE: The doctor said it was a bad case of author-itis.

What do you call a veterinarian with laryngitis?
A hoarse doctor.

PSYCHIATRIST: The last ten sessions you failed to remember any of your dreams. How about today?
PATIENT: Well, last night I dreamed I fell into a vat of cement.
PSYCHIATRIST: Good—finally something concrete!

The dentist asked the absentminded professor, "Would you like some gas?"
"Yes," replied the professor. "Fill 'er up and don't forget to check the oil."

ABSENTMINDED PROFESSOR: Can you tell me where to find the acetyl salicylic acid?

PHARMACIST: Oh, you mean aspirin?

ABSENTMINDED PROFESSOR: Yes, I can never remember that name.

TOP: I once saw a marching band made up of dentists.

TIP: What do you call that?

TOP: A drill squad.

DENTIST: Let me know if I hurt you.

PATIENT: Don't worry, I'll let everybody know.

PATIENT: Doctor, Doctor, I think I'm a fish. Am I crazy?

DOCTOR: Well, now that you mention it, you do look a little green around the gills.

DENTIST: Okay, Bobby, now what kind of filling do you want?

BOBBY: How about chocolate custard?

PATIENT: Doctor, Doctor, I think I'm the world's greatest wrestler.

DOCTOR: Oh, get a grip on yourself.

PATIENT: Doctor, Doctor, what am I allergic to?

DOCTOR: Paying my bills.

DOCTOR: You say you've had this problem for twenty-four hours? Why didn't you come sooner?

PATIENT: I did. That's how long I've been out in the waiting room.

PATIENT: Doctor, Doctor, last night I dreamed I was the world's best fisherman.

DOCTOR: Stay away from me. I don't want to catch anything.

7 Polly Want a Crackup?

What is a woodpecker's favorite side dish?
Beaked potatoes.

Why was the fish asked to leave the movie theater?
He just couldn't shad up.

What's a cow's favorite party game?
Moo-sical chairs.

What is it called when ten toads sit on top of each other?
A toad-em pole.

Why did the haddock and salmon get married?
They were hooked on each other.

Where do the best owl soccer players end up?
In the Owl-Star Game.

What rabbit cheats at blind man's bluff?
Peeker Cottontail.

What's big, gray, and misses all his calls?
An elephant with a broken answering machine.

Whale Tales

What do you get when you cross a whale with a carpenter?
Moby-Deck.

What do you get when you cross a whale with a plumber?
Moby-Drip.

RUDY: Did Moby-Dick cry?
TRUDY: Of course, he whaled all night.

Why did the firefly want to become a maid?
She thought she would be good at light housework.

MANDY: What's worse than a giraffe with a sore neck?
SANDY: A millipede with athlete's foot.

LLOYD: What's gray, weighs five tons, and is covered
with tomato sauce and pepperoni?
FLOYD: An Italian circus elephant.

What has wings and goes "snap, crackle, pop"?
A firefly with a short circuit.

TEACHER: Who can tell me why elephants have ivory
tusks?
CLASS CLOWN: Because iron tusks would rust.

What's gray and white and squishy?
An elephant hiding in a bag of marshmallows.

JILL: The other day I saw an elephant hitchhiking.
PHIL: Now, that's what I call a two-ton pickup.

What do you do with a squeaking elephant?
Give it some peanut oil.

Why did the lion feel sick after he'd eaten the preacher?
Because it's hard to keep a good man down.

How does a bird with a broken wing manage to land safely?
With its sparrow-chute.

SLIM: What kind of bears like to go out in the rain?
TIM: Drizzly bears.

What does a cat sleep on?
A caterpillow!

What do you call a guard with a hundred legs?
A sentry-pede!

What has six legs, bites, and talks in code?
A Morse-quito!

What did the spider say to the fly?
"I'm getting married. Do you want to come to the webbing?"

What kind of bird eats the same worm over and over again?
A sparrow with hiccups.

What great pig spouted philosophy?
Sow-crates.

Why did the rattlesnake go to the emergency room?
He bit his lip.

What's harder than making a giraffe gargle?
Making an elephant take nose drops.

How do eels shop?
Usually, with a charge card.

Did you hear about the angry skunk farmer? He raised a real stink.

What do you call a grizzly who doesn't tell the truth?
A bear-faced liar.

LLOYD: When will an elephant come into your house?
FLOYD: When you leave the pet door open.

What do you call a bee who drops his honey?
A spilling bee.

How is a bee who misplaced his nectar like a girl who lost her boyfriend at the mall?
They're both looking for their honey.

What do bees do with their honey?
Cell it!

What is the rodent capital of Russia?
Mouse-cow.

Where did the fish get his degree?
From a tuna-versity.

JASON: What is a fish's favorite game?
MASON: Salmon Says.

What happened to the oyster on the witness stand?
He clammed up.

FUZZY: I lost my fish. What should I do?
WUZZY: Have you checked the lost-and-flounder department?

What do you call an Australian mammal who swallows pediatricians?
A doc-filled platypus.

What do you get when you cross a duck with a swamp?
Quack-sand.

What do you get when you cross a pumpkin and a duck?

A quack-o'lantern.

Why do penguins have such a hard time getting married?

Every time they march down the aisle, they get cold feet.

What sharp-witted fish is known to his friends as a real cutup?

The swordfish.

**Sign in a Veterinarian's
Waiting Room**

BE BACK IN FIVE MINUTES. SIT! STAY!

What's a penguin's favorite treat at Mexican restaurants?

En-chill-adas.

What's a little weasel's favorite carnival ride?

The ferret's wheel.

How did the three little pigs get around the hospital?

In squeal chairs.

Where do pigs go on vacation?

To the Sows Pacific.

What Vienna boar was a great psychiatrist?

Pigmund Freud.

Why did the silly leopard wear a bib?
He was afraid of getting spots on his coat.

Knock-knock!
Who's there?
Nemo.
Nemo who?
Nemo time to get ready!

What would you get if you crossed a politician with a shark?
A senator who talks your ears, arms, and legs off.

What would you get if you crossed Dracula with a shark?
I'm not sure, but I wouldn't go swimming after dark!

What do you get when you cross a watch with a snail?
Slime time!

MIA: I crossed a suit with a howling monster.
TIA: What did you get?
MIA: A wash-and-werewolf.

Why do lobsters have short tempers?
Because they're always getting steamed.

Where are the fastest chickens at the supermarket?
In the eggs-press aisle.

What kind of amphibian tells jokes?
A silly-mander.

What kind of fires do turtles fear the most?
House fires.

What's gray, weighs three tons, and goes around and around?
A hippo on a carousel.

What's black and white and carries a paddle?
A Ping-Ponguin.

FLIP: What's a shark's favorite type of gumball candy?
FLOP: Jaws Breakers.

What dinosaur was known for killing conversations?
Tyranna-bore-us.

8 Prime Crime

PRISON WARDEN: From now on, it's bread and water for you. How do you like that?

PRISONER: I'd like the bread toasted and the water sparkling.

Why don't they serve chocolate in prison?
Because it makes you break out!

Two burglars broke into a high-rise apartment building. Suddenly, as they snuck into one of the apartments, the first burglar heard a noise. "I think someone's coming. Quick, out the window!"

"Are you crazy?" said the second burglar. "We're on the thirteenth floor!"

Replied the first burglar, "This is no time to be superstitious!"

SLIM: Did you hear about the big robbery at the fish market?

JIM: Yes, the police are launching a full-scale investigation.

Did you hear about the school for junior liars?
They have double-crossing guards.

Where did the judge send the dishonest proofreader?
To a house of corrections.

How are burglars and flies alike?
They're always on the lookout for the swat team.

KERRY: Did you hear about the dog who was caught counterfeiting dollar bills?
TERRY: No.
KERRY: The cops reported that his buck was worse than his bite.

SHERLOCK HOLMES: The murderer lives in the house with the yellow door.
DR. WATSON: That's amazing, Holmes. How did you deduce that?
SHERLOCK HOLMES: It's a lemon entry, my dear Watson.

Did you hear about the world's dumbest detective?
He got on a bicycle built for two and thought someone was following him.

Books from the Jailhouse Library

Searching for Freedom, by Anita File

America's Toughest Jail, by Al Katras

Planning a New Trial, by Noah Lawyer

Discovering Your Cell Isn't Locked, by Ron A. Whey

POLICE CHIEF TO ROOKIE: You call that a police dog? He's the mangiest, dirtiest, scrawniest animal I've ever seen.
ROOKIE: Shhhh! He's working undercover.

The fish-and-game warden caught a fisherman red-handed.
"What's the big idea fishing with last year's license?" snapped the warden.
"Don't worry," the angler replied. "I'm only after the ones I didn't catch last year."

PRISONER: Doctor, my head won't stop hurting.
PRISON DOCTOR: Why don't you take something?
PRISONER: I did. That's why I'm in here.

ABSENTMINDED PROFESSOR: Officer, someone stole my wallet.
POLICE OFFICER: Did you feel a hand in your pocket?
ABSENTMINDED PROFESSOR: Yes, but I thought it was mine.

Why did they make a skunk the sheriff?
The townsfolk were looking for some law and odor.

What happened to the police sketch artist?
He disappeared without a trace.

What did the security guard at the greenhouse say when he heard a noise?
"Halt! Who grows there?"

What do you get when you cross a chicken with a crook?
A peck-pocket.

JOE: Did you hear about the mean mallard who held up a bank?
MOE: Now that's what I call a real robber duckie.

JILL: What paleontologist loved detective cartoons?
DILL: Dig Tracy.

What Old West sheriff never said much?
Quiet Earp.

Knock-knock!
Who's there?
Police.
Police who?
Police and thank you are very nice words.

Did I Mention Detention?

Why was the magnet sent to detention?
Because of his negative attitude.

MYRNA: What are you reading?
VERNA: It's a murder mystery that takes place in a maze.
MYRNA: Is it good?
VERNA: Yeah, but it has a lot of weird twists and turns.

TEACHER: What's mysterious, cold, and once you go there you never come back?
JOKER: The Brrrrrrr-muda Triangle.

HEALTH TEACHER: Is chicken soup good for your health?
HEALTH CLOWN: Not if you're the chicken!

TED: My school is so strict, we have to wear a suit and tie at all times.
NED: Wow, swim class must be a real challenge!

RICH: Hooray! Our geometry teacher is out sick today.
MITCH: What happened?
RICH: She got a sprained angle.

The food in our school cafeteria is so bad, the rats are phoning out for pizza.

DIT: Teacher, I spent eight hours over my math book last night.

TEACHER: You did?

DIT: Yes, it fell under my bed.

FATHER: I just received a note from your teacher saying you're not giving 100 percent at school.

SON: Nonsense . . . on Monday I gave 13 percent, Tuesday 27 percent, Wednesday 35 percent, Thursday 20 percent, and Friday 5 percent.

MATH TEACHER: If your uncle owed one hundred dollars to the grocer, seven hundred dollars to the landlord, and eighty dollars to the doctor, what would all this add up to?

MATH CLOWN: A big headache. He just lost his job.

TEACHER: I just tore this paper into four pieces. What do I have?

CLASS CLOWN: Quarters.

TEACHER: Very good. What do I have if I tear it into eight pieces?

CLASS CLOWN: Eighths.

TEACHER: And if tear it into a hundred pieces?

CLASS CLOWN: Then you have confetti!

Knock-knock!
Who's there?
Harmony.
Harmony who?
Harmony times I got to tell you the school bus is coming?

MANDY: How was the exam on classical composers?

ANDY: Not too bad. It turned out to be an open Bach test.

Grammar Guffaws

TEACHER: Billy, use the word *ammonia* in a sentence.

BILLY: My friend's mom offered me a lift after school, but I said ammonia short way from home.

TEACHER: Daffy, use the word *forfeit* in a sentence.

DAFFY: A horse runs better on forfeit than on two.

TEACHER: José, use the word *antidotes* in a sentence.

JOSÉ: My uncle Jeff likes me, but my antidotes on me.

TEACHER: Lily, use the word *avenue* in a sentence.

LILY: I avenue bicycle.

TEACHER: Fuzzy, what would you like to do today?
FUZZY: Graduate?

What is the study of back-to-school shopping called?
Buy-ology!

Knock-knock!
Who's there?
10-Q.
10-Q who?
10-Q very much, I'm sure.

Why did the teacher bring crackers to his meeting?
Because it was a parrot-teacher conference!

TEACHER: We start class promptly at eight o'clock.
CLASS CLOWN: That's okay. If I'm not here by then, you can start without me.

SCIENCE TEACHER: Jody, what does it mean when the barometer falls?
JODY: It means someone did a lousy job of hanging it up.

How do you save a kid struck down on the playground?
Mouth-to-mouth recess-itation.

Knock-knock!
Who's there?
Formosa.
Formosa who?
Formosa the day, I just watch TV.

New Computer Viruses—How to Tell if Your Computer's Been Hit!

School.nurse virus—it automatically dials your parents to pick you up.

Cheerleader.virus.rah—it doesn't really do anything except encourage other viruses.

Party.virus—it crashes your computer and your parties.

PRINCIPAL TO NEW STUDENT: I hope you're not one of those students who sits and watches the school clock.

THE NEW PUPIL: No, sir. I've got a digital watch that beeps at three fifteen.

LAFFY: What shall we play today?

DAFFY: How about we play school?

LAFFY: That's a great idea. You be the teacher and I'll be absent.

TIMMY: Hi, Mom. Sorry I'm late. I had to stay after school again.

MOM: For crying out loud!

TIMMY: No, for laughing out loud.

UNCLE HARRY: Well, Billy, do you like your new school?

BILLY: Sometimes.

UNCLE HARRY: And when is that?

BILLY: When it's closed!

LEM: I can't go out and play after school.

CLEM: Why not?

LEM: Because I promised Dad that I would stay in and help him with my homework.

TEACHER: Why are you always staring out the window?

CLASS CLOWN: I'm working on becoming a television weatherman.

MOM: Why were you kicked out of barber school?

TOM: I cut too many classes and not enough hair.

10 Fizz-Ed!

What kind of carts do golfers need?
Carts equipped with fore-wheel drive.

Why was the cop fired from his part-time job at the bowling alley?
He kept giving tickets for changing lanes.

What section of the airplane do martial arts experts prefer?

Fist class.

What did the dogsled racer win?

A cold medal.

What gets harder to catch the faster you run?

Your breath.

Why did the dumb football player bring a microwave onto the field?

He thought the coach announced, "Two-minute warming."

What do computers and great tennis teams have in common?

Really good servers.

Games They Play

Chimney sweepers play sootball.

Bees play hive-and-seek.

Farmers play field hockey.

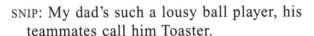

SNIP: My dad's such a lousy ball player, his
teammates call him Toaster.
SNAP: Why is that?
SNIP: Because every time it's his turn at bat, he pops
up.

What do you call a golfer who hits balls out of the car?
A backseat driver.

Why did the baseball coach bring a boa constrictor to the game?
He thought he could pull off a squeeze play.

11 Tasty Tickles

Knock-knock!
  Who's there?
Possum.
  Possum who?
Possum ketchup on my cheeseburger!

What do you call a town with two million fresh eggs?
  New Yolk City!

What would you get if you crossed a candle maker with a dieter?

Someone who can really burn calories.

CHAD: Why don't you peel the banana before eating it?

BRAD: Why should I? I already know what's inside.

What did the buttered toast wear to bed?

A pair of jam-mies.

What would you get if you crossed an ice cream drink with a cobra?

A malted milk snake.

DINER: Waiter, is there a fly in my soup?

WAITER: Oh, no, that's vitamin bee.

DANA: What goes "A B C D E F G H I J K L M— slurp, slurp"?

LANA: A kid eating half a bowl of alphabet soup.

DINER: I had the bison steak. How much do I owe you?

WAITER: I don't know. Let me get you the Buffalo Bill.

Sign on a Pizza Delivery Van

SEVEN DAYS WITHOUT PIZZA MAKES
ONE WEAK.

What do cannibals call five scouts and their leader?

A snack pack.

NUTRITION TEACHER: Give me an example of a balanced diet.

CLASS CLOWN: A cupcake in each hand.

One day Zed was waiting in line at a pizza shop when he noticed a little old lady staring at him. After a while, the woman said, "Forgive me, but you look just like my son who moved cross country. I know this sounds silly, but it would make me so happy if you called out, 'Good-bye, Mother,' just as I leave. Would you do that?"

"Sure," said Zed. "Anything to make you happy." So he did.

As Zed approached the checkout counter, the clerk smiled and said, "That'll be twenty dollars."

"Wait a minute!" complained Zed. "All I ordered was a slice."

"Yeah, I know," returned the clerk. "But your mom said you'd pay for her two pies."

Dessert Dillies

Gossip columnists love spice cake.

Ministers love angel food cake.

Lumberjacks love Black Forest cake.

Rabbits love carrot cake.

Dogcatchers love pound cake.

Elves love shortcake.

Little Jimmy was invited to his friend Harry's birthday party. After the party was over, Harry's mother said to Jimmy, "Why don't you have some more candy and cookies?"

"No, thanks," said Jimmy politely. "I'm full."

"Well, then," said Harry's mother, "why don't you fill your pockets with candies to eat on the way home?"

"No, thanks," Jimmy repeated. "My pockets are full, too."

VINNY: My dad just opened a candy business.
WINNIE: I bet he makes a mint.

What is red and green and goes up and down?
A tomato in an elevator!

Who flies through the air with an umbrella and makes corn kernels jump?
Mary Pop-Pop-Pop-pins.

Why was the mermaid thrown out of the chorus?
She couldn't carry a tuna.

Harvey walked into a restaurant and ordered a cup of hot chocolate. When it arrived, he promptly poured it into a plant and ate the cup and saucer, leaving only the handle.

"More!" ordered Harvey. As the waiter brough more and more hot chocolate, Harvey repeated the process until the table was full of nothing but cup handles.

"I guess you must think I'm crazy, huh?" said Harvey to the waiter.

"I certainly do," replied the waiter. "The handle's the best part."

Sign in a Restaurant Window

DON'T STAND THERE AND BE HUNGRY,
COME ON IN AND GET FED UP.

What is a comic's favorite snack?
Corn bread.

CUSTOMER: Waiter, there's a fly in my soup.
WAITER: Don't worry; the spider crawling over your spoon will eat it.

TIP: Do you enjoy making hamburgers at work?
TOP: Nah, every day it's the same old grind.

Dumbest Fast-Food Joke in the World

A hot dog and a hamburger fell out the back of a fast-food delivery truck. Which was hurt the most?

The hamburger, because the burger they are, the furter they fall.

COOKING STUDENT: Oh, I want to become a chef in the worst way.

INSTRUCTOR: After tasting your meat loaf, I'd say you've made it.

What do oranges and electrical outlets have in common?

A lot of juice.

WAITER: George Washington once dined at this very table.

DINER: Is that why you haven't changed the tablecloth since?

DINER: Waiter, there are fifty flies in my soup.

WAITER: Congratulations! You're the first customer to do that without a calculator.

DINER: Waiter, there's a snail in my chop suey.

WAITER: Oh, that's nothing. Wait till you see what's in your fortune cookie.

DINER: Waiter, why are there so many ants in my soup?
WAITER: Because we ran out of bug spray and decided
to drown them instead.

A diner trying to eat a meal found himself annoyed by
a violinist who played the same tune over and over.
"Excuse me," said the customer, "don't you know
how to play anything else?"
"Of course, sir," replied the violinist. "What would
you like me to play?"
"How about a nice quiet game of chess?" said the
customer.

What do you get when you cross a hot pepper with a pickle?
A fire dill.

BILLY: Did you hear about the new parachute diet?
JILLY: No.
BILLY: It's incredible how fast your weight drops.

What's a rich kid's favorite snack?
Fortune cookies.

Did you hear about the new jump-rope diet?
To lose weight, you just skip dessert.

What kind of crackers do firefighters like in their
soup?
Firecrackers!

What Chinese soup makes you sleepy?
Yawn-ton soup.

What do you eat at a church picnic?
Hymn-burgers!

What do you call artificial spaghetti?
Mock-aroni!

What's brown, hairy, and wears sunglasses?
A coconut on summer vacation!

When do you stop at green and go at red?
When you're eating a watermelon!

What happened to the young chef who missed cooking class?
He had a lot of homework to ketchup on!

What type of cheese do dogs like on their pizza?
Mutts-arella!

What do you get when you cross a fire-breathing dragon with a chicken?
Hot wings!

Why did the orange stop in the middle of the road?
Because he ran out of juice.

What is green with red spots?
A pickle with measles!

A man went into the slowest-serving restaurant in the world and waited an hour for the waitress. An hour later, the appetizers were served. Then an hour later came the dinner entrée.

A long time later, the waitress finally came back with the check and asked, "Is there anything else?"

"Yes," replied the man. "Breakfast."

12. Ghoulish Giggled

JASON: Why do vampires have such a high divorce rate?

MASON: Things never seem to work out when your love is in vein.

What do you call a scary movie about a monster who takes money?
The Bribe of Frankenstein.

What happened to Godzilla after he chewed through the streets of New York?
He came down with a sewer throat.

Did you hear about the skeleton who went on a low-fat milk diet? Now he's all skim and bones.

What country produces the most hypnotists?
Trance-sylvania, of course!

What do you get when you cross a hen with a ghost?
Fright chicken.

What's a zombie's favorite food?
Chicken croak-ettes.

How did Electro-Man get elected president of all superheroes?
He got all the volts.

STU: What side of Godzilla should you stay away from?
LOU: The inside.

What is a ghoul's favorite flower?
Morning gories.

MINDY: Yesterday I took my boyfriend to see the Monster from the Mucky Marsh.
CINDY: What was he like?
MINDY: Oh, about ten feet tall, with a horrible, slimy head, and big yellow teeth.
CINDY: I don't mean your boyfriend; what was the monster like?

Why are robots never afraid?
Because they have nerves of steel.

What do you get if you cross a duck with Dracula?
Count Down.

How does a witch doctor ask a girl to dance?
"Voodoo like to dance with me?"

What do you get when you cross a magician with playground equipment?
Somebody who seesaws girls in half.

What computer browser do witches use?
Internet Hex-plorer.

What do you call a gremlin on crutches?
A hobblin' goblin.

What did the witch cry when her coffeemaker blew up?
  "Brew-hoo!"

CHUCKIE: Do werewolves ever argue?
BUCKIE: Whenever there's a full moon, they fight tooth
  and nail.

What do you get when you cross Junior Birdman with
a tow-truck driver?
  Somebody real good at fixing flap tires.

MONSTER: Will this hurt?
DR. FRANKENSTEIN: Let's just say you're in for a big
  shock.

What do vampires wear in the fall?
  Their bat-to-school clothes!

What did the monster get when he won the race?
A ghoul medal.

What is red with green spots?
I don't know, but whatever it is, it just crawled behind your ear.

What's a ghost's favorite dog?
A ghoul-den retriever!

What do ghosts like on their bagels?
Scream cheese.

ZIP: Last night I had a nightmare about a giant monster dog.

ZAP: You must have been terrier stricken.

Where does the Green Goblin fill his gas tank?
At the villain station.

Computer Sign of the Times

SCOTTISH LAKE MONSTER INTERNET SERVICE—BE THE FIRST TO LOCH ON.

What's green, crunchy, and bites you on the neck?
A vampickle.

Who created the fowlest monster in the world?
Ducktor Frankenstein.

What goes "Flap! Flap! Bite! Bite! Ouch! Ouch!"
Dracula with a toothache.

SLIM: What's the difference between a Little Leaguer, a major leaguer, and Dracula?

TIM: A Little Leaguer has an aluminum bat, a major leaguer has a wooden bat, and Dracula has a vampire bat.

What do you get when a ghost sits in a tree?
Petrified wood!

Why did the monster eat the North Pole?
He was in the mood for a frozen dinner!

What kind of streets do ghosts like to gather on?
Dead-end streets!

Cold Cases

JILL: How do you know when a vampire has raided your refrigerator?

PHIL: There are bite marks in your ketchup container.

DILLY: How do you know when a werewolf has raided your refrigerator?

DALLY: There are paw prints in the butter.

PHILLY: How do you know when a mummy has raided your refrigerator?

MILLI: All the food is unwrapped!

What would happen if pigs could fly?
Bacon would go up.

What position did the zombie play on the baseball team?
Dead center field.

Sign in an Egyptian History Museum

SATISFACTION
GUARANTEED
OR
DOUBLE YOUR
MUMMY BACK.

LAFFY: Did you hear that the ghosts at the factory went on strike?
DAFFY: Yes, but management hired a skeleton crew.

What got the fisherman in trouble?
He sold his sole to the devil.

What kind of gills are French fishermen afraid of?
Gill-otines.

DILL: How can you tell when a vampire has sneaked into a bakery?
WILL: All the filling from the jelly doughnuts is missing.

What magazine do ghosts love to read?
Good Housecreeping.

What kind of yard sales attract zombies?
Grave-yard sales.

What would you get if you crossed a practical joker with a mad scientist?
Dr. Prankenstein.

Sign in Front of a Mortuary

DRIVE CAREFULLY. WE'LL WAIT.

Why do ghosts make such poor football fans?
They spend all their time booing!

What kind of art are ghosts good at?
Ghoulages.

What overnight shipping company do vampires use?
Necks Day Delivery.

Last Laughs

Knock-knock!
Who's there?
Overalls.
Overalls who?
Overalls, this is the best joke book I've ever read!

MINA: How do you tell a boomerang good-bye?
TINA: You say, "Many happy returns."

Index.